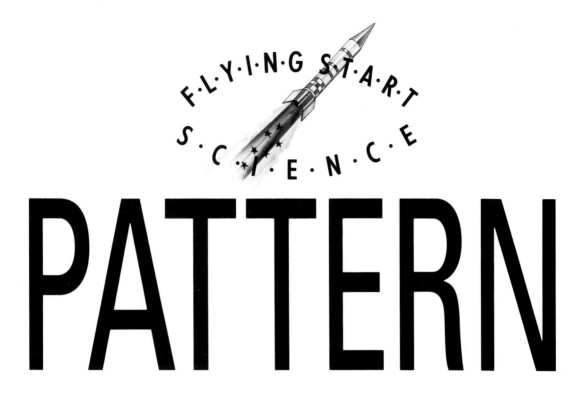

PATTERN

Written and photographed by

Kim Taylor

John Wiley & Sons, Inc.

New York · Chichester · Brisbane · Toronto · Singapore

Contents

Designed by **Kate Buxton, Times Four Publishing Ltd**

Illustrated by **Chris Lyon**

Science adviser: **Richard Oels**

First published in the U.K. by Belitha Press Limited 1992.

Copyright © In this format Belitha Press Limited and Times Four Publishing 1992.

US edition first published by John Wiley & Sons, Inc. 1992.

Text © Kim Taylor/Times Four Publishing Ltd 1992.
Photographs © Kim Taylor 1992 (except where credited elsewhere)
Design and illustration © Belitha Press and Times Four Publishing Ltd 1992.

Origination by Bright Arts, Hong Kong
Typeset by Amber Graphics, Burgess Hill

ISBN 0-471-57982-3

The publisher and the author have made every reasonable effort to ensure that the experiments and activities in this book are safe when conducted as instructed but assume no responsibility for any damage caused or sustained while performing the experiments or activities in this book. Parents, guardians, and/or teachers should supervise young readers who undertake the experiments and activities in this book.

Printed in China for Imago

About this book

There are patterns all around us, in the natural world of plants and animals (like the fish scales seen here) and in things that humans make. There are patterns in our homes, on walls, floors and fabrics. Once you become aware of patterns you will begin to see them in all sorts of places.

Patterns often have a purpose. In the animal world, for example, body patterns can help creatures to signal to each other or hide from enemies. People invent patterns that may be useful – or they may simply be good to look at. The fascinating photographs in this book will give you some idea of the variety of patterns to be seen.

Throughout the book there are simple experiments for you to try so you can find out more.

CAUTION: You may need to ask an adult to help with the cutting in the experiments which require the use of scissors or a knife.

What is a pattern?

Patterns are arrangements of shape or color. If you put a blob of paint on a piece of paper, you might call it a very simple sort of pattern. If you put more blobs of the same shape at **regular** intervals all over the paper you have something much closer to what people usually mean by the word pattern. It is when shapes or colors are repeated that we begin to recognize a pattern.

People like to decorate themselves or wear the latest fashions so they are more noticeable. This man from Papua New Guinea is dressed up for a special occasion. He has painted a pattern on his face and is wearing a wig with a bird of paradise feather in it.

Matching halves

The markings on one wing of this moth are a **mirror image** of those on the other wing. This is called a **symmetrical** pattern.

The symmetrical pattern above was made by putting blobs of wet paint on a piece of paper and folding the paper over. The original paint shape got repeated on the other half of the paper, so making a pattern.

4

Natural patterns

The patterns found in nature are rarely exactly regular. The holes and dots on this sea urchin are not spaced evenly, but they make a recognizable pattern.

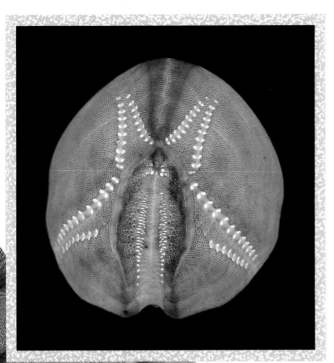

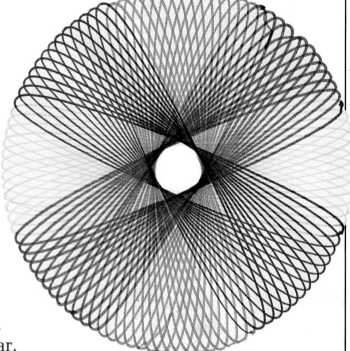

Machine-made patterns

Patterns made by a machine, like this **Spirograph** drawing, are neat and regular.

There are lots of patterns on this house. Some of them simply make the house more attractive. Can you see which ones those are? Other patterns are more useful. The overlapping wall and roof tiles, for example, help to keep the house dry.

Natural patterns

Patterns can be found everywhere in nature, from the coats of spotted Dalmatian dogs to the beautiful markings on some seashells, birds' feathers, flower petals and insect bodies. Each mark is usually a slightly different size, shape and distance from its neighbors.

Did you know?

The colors of rainbows always form the same pattern: red, orange, yellow, green, blue, indigo and violet. Red is usually on the outside edge of the rainbow.

Underwater patterns

These shells and corals from the warm waters of Jamaica have beautiful patterns. No two are exactly the same.

The shells were once the homes of sea creatures. The white corals are the skeletons of creatures that look like sea anemones.

This monarch butterfly from Africa has just hatched out from its **chrysalis**. The white spots on its black body are all slightly different shapes and sizes. The long black curled part on its head is its tongue!

Pine cones are made of overlapping scales, all of a similar shape. As the pine cone opens, the scales separate. The pattern they make is rather like the overlapping tiles on the house shown on page 5.

One day these caterpillars will turn into cinnabar moths. First they must fill themselves with food. With their bold stripes they also make sure that other creatures see them. On pages 18-19 you can find out why this is important.

Pattern experiment

THE COLOR OF SUNLIGHT

You need
- A straight glass
- A jug of water
- A sheet of paper
- A piece of card 2½ × 3½ inches (6 × 9 cm)
- Early morning sunshine

1 Cut the card so it is about half the height of the glass.

2 Stand the glass on the sheet of paper, in low sunlight coming through a window.

3 Lean the card against the glass on the side opposite the sunshine.

4 Pour water into the glass until it is higher than the card. A rainbow should appear in the shadow.

The water bends the light from the sun and breaks it up into its separate colors.
This is called refraction.

Human patterns

People enjoy patterns. They use them to decorate the places they live in and the things they wear. Sometimes they decorate their bodies, too. You can often see patterns in the shape of things that people make, such as buildings and machines. Patterns can be made using machines, or by feeding numbers into a computer. They can also be made using the human eye and artistic talent.

The pattern on the right was produced by a computer, using very complicated sets of numbers that were programmed into it. The result looks rather like a fabric pattern.

The red **geometric** pattern below is from North Africa. The flower pattern is from an old French fabric.

Fabric patterns

People all over the world have invented patterns to weave and dye into **fabrics**. They make the fabric more attractive and unusual.

Street patterns

These paving stones are the same shape and size so they make a regular pattern. The car, seen from above, is symmetrical. Its right side is a mirror image of its left.

Pattern experiment

COLLECTING PATTERNS

You need
- A ring binder
- A hole punch
- Scissors

1 Collect any old pieces of patterned wallpaper and cloth you can find.

2 Cut out pieces you like so they fit the size of the binder and punch holes in them to fit the rings.

3 Sort the patterns into groups in your binder: stripes, dots, rings, flowers. See how many different kinds you can gather in your collection.

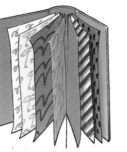

Patterns for fun

Bright patterns cheer people and amuse them. Clowns wear bright patterns and paint their faces to entertain people. Each circus clown has a special face pattern which no other clown may copy.

Radial patterns

A pattern in which everything comes out from a central point, like a drawing of the rays of the sun, is called a **radial** pattern. Wheels with spokes, and some simple animals, form radial patterns. Many flowers also have radial shapes and patterns.

The waterlily (below) and the orange daisy (left) are radial shapes. Each petal radiates out from the center of the flower. This helps to direct bees and other insects to the center, where the sweet **nectar** is.

A radial animal

The **tentacles** of this sea anemone (which is an animal, not a flower) make a pattern that radiates around it. The anemone uses its tentacles to catch small creatures to eat.

The bodies of starfish are shaped in a radial pattern. This enables them to use their "arms" to move in any direction they wish across the seabed.

Pattern experiment

MAKE A PAPER FLOWER

1 Draw a large circle with the compass, or trace around the small plate.

2 Cut out the circle and fold it in half three times.

3 Make six cuts in the folded paper exactly as in the drawing.

4 Open the paper out and you will find a radiating flower pattern.

A dartboard is a familiar radial pattern. It also has a pattern of circles. Players score different points depending on which part of the pattern their dart lands in.

A radial plant

The seeds of this goatsbeard plant are arranged in a **three-dimensional** radial pattern. They radiate in all directions. Each seed has a parachute to carry it away on the wind.

11

Repeating patterns

Repeating patterns are made of the same shapes that are used over and over again. The shapes that are repeated are called **motifs**. The motifs may be exactly the same as each other or there may be small differences between them.

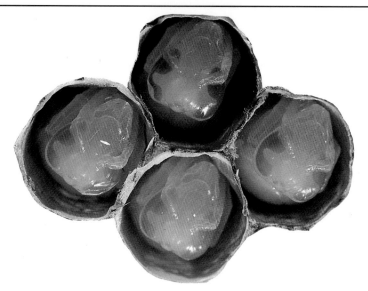

In the fabrics below, the materials have been dyed in various repeating patterns. Which patterns have motifs that are exactly the same as each other? Which patterns have motifs that are similar to each other, but not exactly the same?

There are many repeating patterns in nature, such as these cells in which tree wasp larvae are living. Because they are not quite circular but six-sided, each cell fits in neatly between the others and the available space is used to the full.

The bottles in this rack form a regular repeating pattern when seen end-on. This is a space-saving way to store bottles. Standing them upright would take a lot more space. However, if the bottles were arranged like the wasp cells above, they would fit together more closely, allowing more bottles to be stored in the space available.

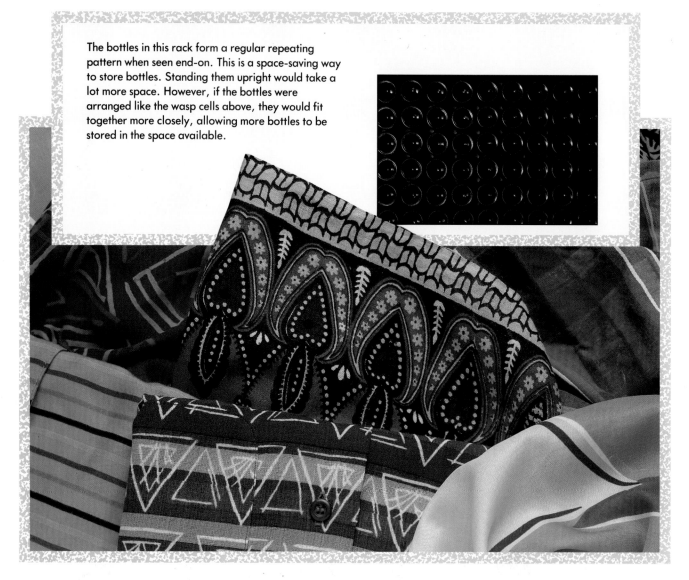

Prickly patterns

This cactus has spines that stick out in little clumps around the fleshy stem. They are repeated all over the stem and help to keep hungry animals away from the plant.

Did you know?

Scottish tartan fabrics are covered in repeating check patterns. There are more than 200 different tartans. Each clan (family) has its own pattern of checks.

Over and over

If you group identical objects together, your eyes may see them as a pattern. One of these pencils on its own does not make a pattern, but a group of them together makes a pattern that repeats over and over.

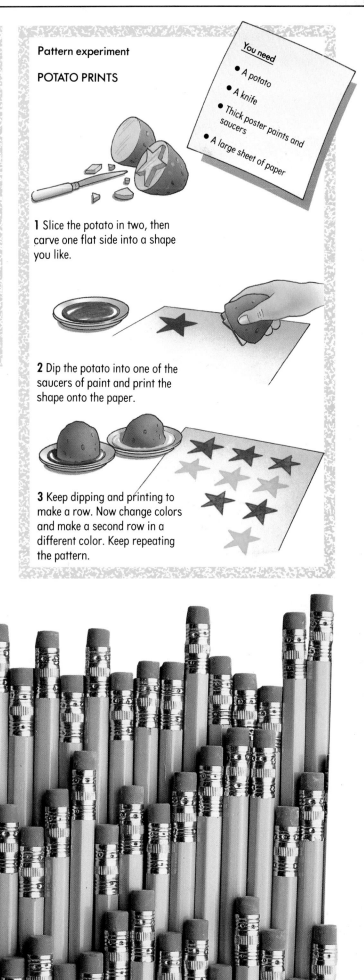

Pattern experiment

POTATO PRINTS

You need
- A potato
- A knife
- Thick poster paints and saucers
- A large sheet of paper

1 Slice the potato in two, then carve one flat side into a shape you like.

2 Dip the potato into one of the saucers of paint and print the shape onto the paper.

3 Keep dipping and printing to make a row. Now change colors and make a second row in a different color. Keep repeating the pattern.

Rings

Ring patterns are made of circles. When the circles all have the same center, the pattern is called **concentric**. An archery target has a pattern of concentric circles. So, too, do tree trunks and the dartboard shown on page 11. The Olympic flag, however, has separate circles each with its own center. You can make patterns like these quite easily with a compass and a pencil.

The five circles of the Olympic flag represent the five continents from which the competitors in the games come. The circles overlap and so are not concentric.

Rings within rings

When something falls into water it makes a pit in the surface. Gravity tries to keep the surface level, so it causes water to rush up to fill the pit. It rushes up so fast that it makes a peak. For a second or so, pits and peaks alternate, sending out ring-shaped ripples. Here, three stones fell into a pond together, so there are three sets of circles.

You need
• A set of concentric circles, as shown here
• A piece of paper with writing on it

1 Hold the book in both hands and look at the spot on the right. Move the book in small circles, first in one direction and then in the other. Can you see the spokes turning inside the rings? Your eyes are seeing a pattern that is not really there.

2 You can get the same effect even when the book is not moving. Place a piece of paper with writing on it in front of the blue spot. Look hard at the paper while turning it in circles and *holding the book still.* The spokes will reappear!

If you cut a tree trunk across, you find a pattern of concentric circles inside. This is because the tree trunk grows one new layer each year around the outside of the previous year's layer. By counting the rings you can work out how old the tree is.

Did you know?

Counting by the rings, the oldest tree known in the world was a giant sequoia of the Sierra Nevada mountains of California. It was over 3500 years old.

This compact disc looks as if it is covered in concentric circles, but it is actually a very fine **spiral** pattern (see pages 28-29). Each ring of the spiral is made up of millions of tiny dots. Light reflected off the disc appears as rainbow colors.

Safe patterns

The natural world is full of danger for those animals that are eaten by others. So the patterns on some creatures' bodies have a very important purpose – to help them hide from **predators**. One way to do this is to look like your surroundings. This is called **camouflage**. Some creatures, such as the chameleon and octopus, can actually change their colors to suite their surroundings.

A black moth, like this one, is an easy target for a hungry bird. But there is another moth on the tree trunk. Can you spot it? It is very well camouflaged. Its pattern is very like the surface of the birch tree trunk it is hiding on.

To see or not to see

This old Soviet plane has a top camouflaged to look like the ground, so it is difficult to see from above. Underneath it is blue, like the sky, so it is hard for a pilot to spot when flying below it. The star and flash show which country it belongs to.

The vanishing snake

The patterns on this puff adder hide its body perfectly on the stony African ground. Its outline is broken up by the different colors of the pattern, so it is hard to see.

SPOT THE MOTH

You need
• Pencil and paper
• Paints or colored pencils
• Reusable adhesive

1 Fold a piece of paper in two and draw six half-moth shapes along the fold, each 1½ inches (4cm) across.

2 Cut out the moth shapes. Color two of them brightly and two dark or black. Give the fifth light spots and the sixth dark spots.

3 Stick all six moths to the same side of a tree trunk.

4 Stand your friends about 20 yards (20m) away and tell them to approach the tree slowly.

How close did they get before they saw all six moths. Which did they see first? Which last? Why?

The octopus can change its color pattern to suit its background. This one is well hidden among the rocks of the seabed.

Did you know?

Many sea fish, like this herring, have silvery sides. These reflect the light underwater like a mirror. This makes the fish difficult for predators to see.

Some insects hide by looking like leaves or twigs. This East African grasshopper looks very like the fruit of the tree where it is hiding.

Dangerous patterns

Not all creatures want to hide from their enemies. Some, like the grasshopper and the toad shown here, actually want to be seen! They are very brightly colored and highly patterned so that every hungry bird or animal will spot them. This is because they are poisonous to eat. They protect themselves from being eaten by advertising this fact with **warning colors** that say "Don't eat me, I'm poisonous!"

If you see an insect or a frog that has a bright red or yellow pattern, it may be poisonous or able to sting you!

The lubber grasshopper from East Africa spreads its orange and yellow wings to warn birds that it is dangerous to eat.

Warning colors

Warning colors are almost always red, orange or yellow. This fire-bellied toad has glands in its skin containing a powerful poison. The bright orange pattern on its belly warns predators to keep away.

People sometimes use colored patterns to change their appearance and make themselves look more fierce. This New Guinea man has painted his face to warn people that he is a powerful warrior.

These berries tell birds when they are ready to eat. Green means unripe (stop); yellow means half ripe (get ready); red means ready (go). Traffic lights use the same colours in reverse. Warning: some berries can be poisonous to people, so never try to eat them.

Pattern experiment

THE FROG THAT MAKES YOU CROAK

1 Fold the paper in half and put a thick blob of red paint in the crease. Squeeze the paper so the paint spreads. Open it up and let it dry.

2 Add small blobs of black, some in the fold, some to one side of it. Squeeze, then open and let dry.

3 Fold the paper again and draw a half frog shape on the side.

4 Cut it out. Then open up your deadly poisonous frog.

Bold red and black markings are signs of danger that all animals recognize and avoid.

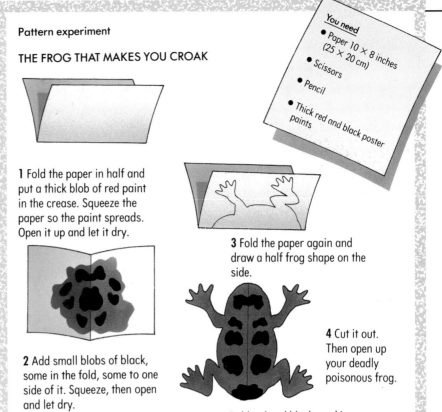

Did you know?

The tiny arrow-poison frog has a venom on its skin so lethal that a single gram can kill 1000 people.

Life size

The cinnabar moth uses its pattern of bright red warning colors to announce to other creatures that it is poisonous. Its caterpillars (see page 7) are also brightly colored for the same reason.

Spots and eyes

Many creatures and flowers have spotted patterns. Spots help animals and plants to survive. Some plants have spotted flowers to attract insects so the plants can reproduce themselves. Some animals have spotted skins as camouflage. Spots can also be used in more unusual ways – to look like eyes and so frighten an animal's enemies.

Attractive spots

The spots on these lilies attract insects and lead them down into the flower to gather nectar. The insects then carry the flower's **pollen** to another flower.

Confusing eyes

The black spot towards the tail of this butterfly fish looks like its eye. Its real eye is hidden by a black stripe.

This confuses predators and helps the fish to escape.

Compare the staring eyes of this owl with the "eyes" on the wings of the moth on the opposite page.

Dangerous eyes

Eye patterns on the wings of this moth look like the eyes of an owl. When a small bird comes near, the moth suddenly opens its wings and displays the "eyes." The little bird is terrified and flies away to look for a meal elsewhere.

1 Look at this pattern of lines closely. At first they seem to form a jumble.

2 Hold the book away from you and rows of spots appear. Can you see how the spots were made without using any curved lines at all?

3 Prop the book open and look at it even further away. Two lines of spots form a V-shape that appears to stand out from the other rows of spots. Can you see why?

4 Spotted patterns trick the eye by drawing attention to themselves and away from the rest of the image.

Did you know?

There are over 140 spots on a peacock's tail. Each spot is the end of a single, long fern-like feather.

No two spots on a leopard's coat are exactly the same. Together they make a **dappled** pattern like light and shade beneath trees. This helps the cat to hide and wait for a good meal to come along!

Stripes

Striped patterns can make objects either easier or more difficult to see. Soft-colored, wavy stripes break up an animal's outline and make it more difficult to see. Bold stripes make it stand out from its background.

People use stripes for similar reasons. Wavy brown and green stripes can help to camouflage tanks and army trucks. Brightly colored stripes on a sports shirt are meant to stand out and make it clear which team the player belongs to.

Stripes for hiding

This animals is called a kudu. It has thin white stripes on its body to break up its outline against a background of trees.

Stripes for display

This angelfish's stripes make it easily recognizable to other fish of its own kind.

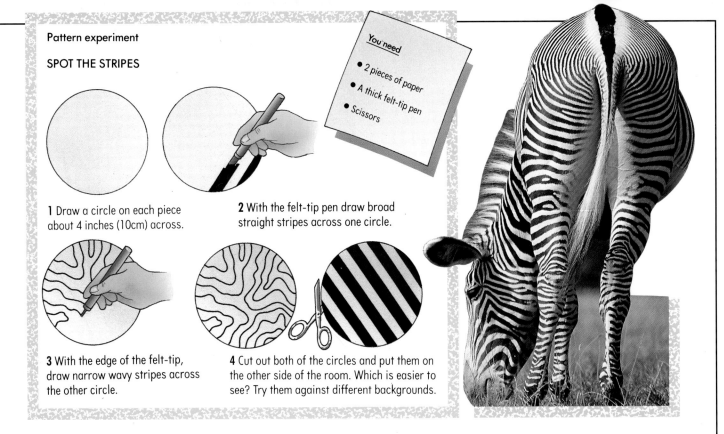

Pattern experiment

SPOT THE STRIPES

1 Draw a circle on each piece about 4 inches (10cm) across.

2 With the felt-tip pen draw broad straight stripes across one circle.

3 With the edge of the felt-tip, draw narrow wavy stripes across the other circle.

4 Cut out both of the circles and put them on the other side of the room. Which is easier to see? Try them against different backgrounds.

Camouflage or display?

This car has been painted like a zebra. Perhaps the pattern would help to camouflage the car on the African grasslands, but in the city it makes it stand out from all the others!

Zebras have wavy stripes that dazzle their enemies and so help them hide on the African grasslands. Each zebra has its own unique pattern of stripes just as each person has his or her own pattern of fingerprints.

Did you know?

Stripes running from side to side make something look wider. Stripes running up and down make an object look taller.

23

Overlapping

Overlapping patterns come from the structure of an object – the way it is made. Tiles on a roof form an overlapping pattern. Because they are laid one over another and on a slope, rainwater runs over them and off the roof without damaging the house beneath. Fish, lizards and snakes have overlapping scales that protect the soft skin underneath. Because the scales are separate and overlap, they also enable the animal to bend its body.

A leafy carpet

If you look closely at this water fern you will see it is made of overlapping sections. This fern grows quickly in summer and covers the surface of ponds with red and green leaves.

Stretchy snakes

The scales on a snake overlap, allowing its body to bend and its skin to stretch when it breathes. If the snake swallows a big meal its skin may stretch so much that the scales separate to form a pattern of diamond shapes.

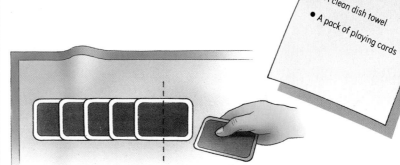

These are the cones of the Douglas fir tree. They are covered in scales, like a large flower bud. This enables the cone to open.

The tiles on this building are more than simply for protection. They have been laid in patterns to make the building attractive.

Pattern experiment

EASY OVER

You need

- A clean dish towel
- A pack of playing cards

1 Place the towel on a table and lay out ten cards in a row, top to bottom and face down. Each one must overlap the next card by at least half its length. The towel keeps the cards from sliding along the table.

2 Carefully turn back the *first* card you placed down, so it lifts the next card and flips it over too. The others will quickly follow until the last one ends face up like the rest.

This experiment shows that by disturbing one part of an overlapping pattern you can change every other part.

Did you know?

Rattlesnakes make their rattling noise by shaking special overlapping scales on their tails.

The millipede is an animal that has a body made of overlapping rings. They enable it to bend. Millipedes can curl up into a spiral shape.

Branching

Branching patterns have sections that get smaller as they grow out from a central structure. For example, trees have trunks from which large branches grow. The branches divide into smaller branches and these divide again into thin twigs. You can see branching in many kinds of plants – in their stems and leaves and in the pattern of veins in the leaves.

People also build branching structures such as television antennas and ships' masts. Even you branch! Your arms and legs are the branches from your body, or trunk, and your fingers and toes are the twigs! Inside, you have branching veins carrying blood around your body.

Here you can see two examples of branching, as the stag's antlers and the trees' branches stand out against the evening sky.

Levels of branching

The differently sized sections of a branching pattern are called "levels" of branching. This fern has three levels of branching – side branches, leaf branches and the small leaves themselves.

Branching veins, similar to veins in the human body, take water and food to all parts of a leaf.

BRANCHING OUT

1 Put the ruler down on a piece of paper. This will be your "tree trunk."

2 Lay whole toothpicks around the ruler to form "branches."

3 Place pieces of toothpick around each whole toothpick to form "twigs."

4 On the paper, draw "leaves" on each twig.

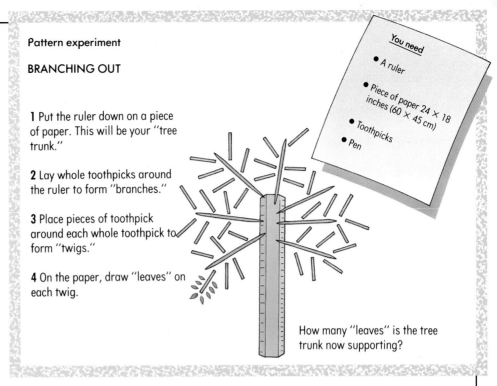

You need
- A ruler
- Piece of paper 24 × 18 inches (60 × 45 cm)
- Toothpicks
- Pen

How many "leaves" is the tree trunk now supporting?

Antenna branches

Television antennas are made of various thicknesses of tubing fixed together. This makes them strong and light. Each level of branching is smaller than the previous one.

Did you know?

A fully grown oak tree can have as many as a quarter of a million leaves. The leaves weigh about 550 pounds (250kg).

Ships' masts make branching patterns like the trunks and branches of trees. This makes them light and yet strong enough to carry the sails. Sailing ships like this one have tall masts with cross-pieces on which the sails are hung. Sailors climb up the masts on rope ladders so they can roll up the sails when gales blow.

Spirals

Spirals are shapes that start at a central point and then go round and round, as rope does when you coil it on the ground. Some creatures have spiral-shaped shells.

Springs, like those found in old-fashioned beds and clocks, are also spiral-shaped. This allows them to stretch and shrink and be springy.

A spiral staircase

Staircases built in a spiral pattern allow you to climb up to the top of a narrow space, such as a tower.

The nautilus shell is made up of many sections joined together. The creature lives inside the biggest section at the end of the spiral. As the creature grows, it builds on another, bigger, section.

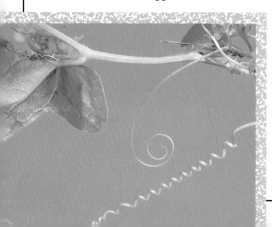

Plant springs

The white bryony plant has spiral **tendrils** to help it climb and cling. They start as flat coils, like the one at the top of the picture. Then they grow into stretchy springs.

Pattern experiment

DRAW A SPIRAL

You need
- Two pencils of the same length
- About 6 inches (15cm) cotton thread
- Tape
- Piece of paper 9 inches (23 cm) square

1 Tape the thread to one pencil as near the *end* as you can, and to the other pencil as near to the *point* as you can, so the pencils are about 4 inches (10 cm) apart.

2 Ask someone to hold the point-up pencil on the middle of the paper. Keep the thread tight as your (point down) pencil draws round theirs.

3 As you draw, your friend will need to change hands so you can get past where their arm is. You should end up drawing a spiral. Can you see why?

Ammonites were creatures with spiral shells that lived in warm seas millions of years ago. They are sometimes found as **fossils**, like these, preserved in ancient rocks.

Did you know?

The Milky Way is a group of more than a billion stars. It has two spiral arms. Our sun is a star on one of the arms.

As a twist drill bites into metal, it pushes out spiral-shaped pieces of waste metal called swarf.

Spiders' webs are not circles but spirals, like the grooves on a record. The spider spins silk from its own body, first building a radiating framework and then spiralling round and round to make a web to catch passing insects to eat.

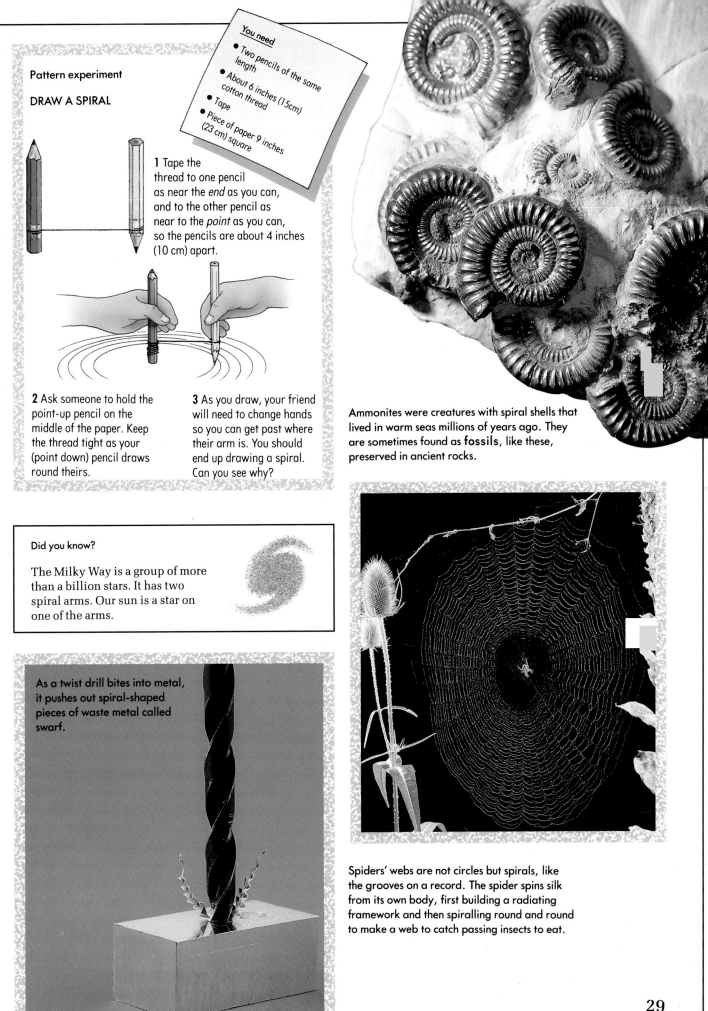

What is it?

Can you work out what each of these patterns is part of? Which ones are human made and which ones belong to the natural world? If you look carefully through the rest of the book you will see some other shapes and patterns that are similar to those on this page.

   The answers are given at the bottom of the page in mirror-writing. Hold the page upside down and up to a mirror to read the answers.

3

2

How many other patterns can you see around you?

7 Lichen plants growing on a rock.
6 The windows of a skyscraper.
5 Fireworks.
4 Cracks in mud.
3 The body of an angelfish.
2 A soap bubble.
1 Painted glass marbles.

Answers

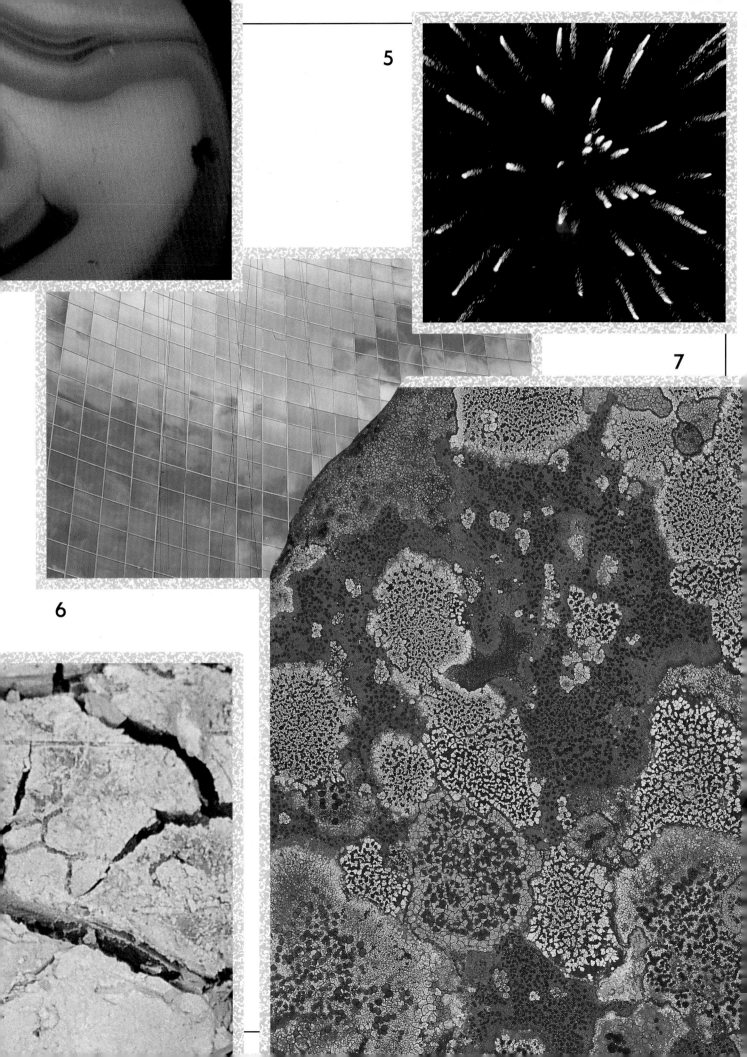

5

7

6

Pattern words

Camouflage Markings that make an animal or object difficult to see.

Chrysalis The resting stage of an insect's life between larva and adult.

Concentric Having the same center.

Dappled Irregularly spotted with dark and light.

Fabric Material, usually woven, that is used to make clothes, furnishings, etc.

Fossils The remains of prehistoric animals and plants found preserved in rocks.

Geometric Made up of shapes such as rectangles, squares and triangles.

Mirror image What an object looks like when seen in a mirror, with left and right reversed.

Motif A shape or mark that is repeated again and again to make a pattern.

Nectar Sweet liquid in flowers that is collected by bees to make honey.

Pollen Fine yellow dust produced by flowers. Pollen has to be carried by insects from one flower to another so that the flowers can produce seeds.

Predators Animals that eat other animals.

Radial Spreading straight out from a central point.

Regular patterns All the same shape.

Repeating patterns One or more shapes shown over and over again.

Spiral Coiling around a center, or winding round and round like the thread of a screw.

Spirograph™ A toy consisting of a set of cog wheels and a frame, used for drawing spiral patterns.

Symmetrical Having identical shapes or patterns similarly placed on opposite sides of a straight line or around a central point.

Tendrils Narrow twisting strands on some plants that help them hold on to a support.

Tentacles Thin, flexible arms used by some animals for holding prey.

Three-dimensional Having length, breadth and depth. A television set, for example, is a three-dimensional box. The pictures on its screen, however, are flat and have no depth. They are only two-dimensional.

Warning colors Color markings on animals that tell other animals that they are dangerous.

Index

PICTURE CREDITS

All photographs are by Kim Taylor and Jane Burton except for Associated Sports Photographs 14 *top;* Kate Buxton 25 *top,* 31 *picture 6;* Bruce Coleman 18 *center;* Eye Ubiquitous 12 *bottom,* 22 *bottom,* 28 *top* and *center;* Hutchison 8 *bottom left* and *right;* Science Photo Library 8 *top;* Zefa *title page,* 4 *top,* 9, 11 *center right,* 12 *center,* 13 *bottom,* 16 *center,* 20 *bottom left,* 23 *center,* 27, 30-31 *picture 1.*